THE ART OF BRAZILIAN ARCHITECTURE

Joaquim Nabuco

Schiffer Publishing Ltd
4880 Lower Valley Road • Atglen, PA 19310

THE ART OF BRAZILIAN ARCHITECTURE

Photos by Joaquim Nabuco

ARCHITECTS

Hélio Pellegrino
James Lawrence Vianna
Ronaldo Fontainha
Sylvia Moura
Paulo de Hungria Machado
Alcides da Rocha Miranda
Oscar Niemeyer

INTERIOR DESIGNERS

Vivi Nabuco
Maria Pia Marcondes Ferraz

LANDSCAPE DESIGNERS

Fernando Chacel
Sônia Infante
Antônio Azeredo

ARTISTS

Cristina Motta
Carina Bokel
Le Corbusier
Hans J. Wegner
Ana Mello Franco
Márcia Grostein
Luiz Aquila
Tuta Espírito Santo

ART BY THE

SEA

Pedro Chermont's House

Hélio Pellegrino

ARCHITECT

HÉLIO PELLEGRINO is a multidisciplinary artist, an architect, interior designer, painter, sculptor, and craftsman. He mixes architecture with painting and handcrafted objects to create harmonious settings where ceilings, walls, and floors become works of art. His projects include crafting personalized lighting fixtures, furniture, sinks, floors, and panels.

PELLEGRINO is a proponent of recycling materials like vintage windows and doors from demolitions of old houses.

He has a passion for Búzios, a charming resort town on the northern coast of Rio de Janeiro, where he participated in the town's architectural makeover. He also developed projects for numerous homes, hotels, restaurants, nightclubs, and shopping malls in and around Búzios, including the Pérola Design Hotel shown below.

Pedro Chermont's House

At Pedro Chermont's home on Ferradura Beach in Búzios, Pellegrino created a privacy wall next to the pool which portrays various sports enjoyed by Chermont's family members.

The wooden fish came from the town of Prados in the state of Minas Gerais, well-known as a community of Brazilian wood sculptors.

Pérola Design Hotel

The Pérola Design Hotel in Búzios is one of Hélio Pellegrino's masterpieces. Since the property is located in a busy area of the town's business district, Pellegrino designed an oval building, a "uterus" as the artist describes it, turned inward with pools and little islands with palm trees. *Pérola* is Portuguese for "pearl," a treasured gem made by oysters inside their shells, a concept echoed by the design of the hotel.

The hotel reception area has a sculpture of a flying woman between a spiral light fixture, symbolizing the sun, and a convex mirror, symbolizing an eye.

Pellegrino also designed the interior and all the paintings, panels, floors, and sculptures, including *Don Quixote* and *Ballerinas*.

Luis Alfeu's House
Pellegrino's work often features the use of alternative and recycled materials. At the home of Luis Alfeu, on Ferradura Beach in Búzios, he designed a thatched roof using an antique iron ratchet wheel from an old sugar mill as the rafters. He also created a light fixture made of dried sea sponges.

Helio Viana's House
Pellegrino is the author of projects and plans in various parts of Brazil and abroad. With one exception, this book focuses on Pellegrino's work in Búzios, a charming coastal resort 200 kilometers (~125 miles) from Rio.
The exception is the home of businessman Hélio Viana, a Pellegrino-designed abode located atop a mountain in the city of Rio de Janeiro. From its position in the neighborhood of Joá, the home has panoramic views of the Barra and Joatinga beaches. The house is famous in Rio and has served as a stage for memorable parties, photo essays, and film productions.
The tall blue doors in the middle of the glass wall came from an ancient church in the state of Bahia.

The Architect's House
Pellegrino's own beach house on Ferradura Beach in Búzios is also his atelier, where he spends his weekends painting and creating new works. The house features several of his sculptures, such as *Kaleidoscope* (page 46 and 50), and *Hamster-Man* (page 47).

PLEYEL

Lagoinha Gated Community
The Lagoinha gated community is located on Ponta da Lagoinha in Búzios. Pellegrino designed unique façades with large doors and round windows.

Boom Restaurant
Pellegrino created a unique light fixture with bottles that, along with the delicious food, is the main attraction at Boom in downtown Búzios. The interior decoration has since been changed by the architect himself, but the light fixture is still there.

"People always ask me if I drank all those bottles dry before creating this chandelier. Actually, my main concern was to help preserve the planet."

Hélio Pellegrino

DEVASSA
Almadén
Red Label
José Cuervo Especial

WOODEN MA

STERPIECES

James Lawrence Vianna

ARCHITECT

Vivi Nabuco
Sylvia Moura

INTERIOR DESIGNERS

Fernando Chacel

LANDSCAPE DESIGNER

Log houses were originally built in cold climates. The challenge proposed by architect JAMES LAWRENCE VIANNA was to adapt the style for homes in a tropical climate. The first step was to open the house through verandahs, internal patios, and glass walls. The roofs did not need a very steep angle either, since Brazil has no snow to run off. Another innovation was to paint the doors with various vibrant colors.

The interior designs were done by VIVI NABUCO and SYLVIA MOURA and the landscaping was by FERNANDO CHACEL, who succeeded in establishing a seamless flow between the gardens and the surrounding forest. The log houses are located outside Rio de Janeiro on the Santa Mathilde and Provence farms in Serra do Brejal.

James Lawrence Vianna designed three logs houses on the Santa Mathilde Farm for Vivi Nabuco and her two daughters, Lúcia and Sylvia. The first log house belongs to Vivi, who did the interior design. The duck on the verandah was sculpted in wood in the village of Bichinho, near the heritage town of Tiradentes in the state of Minas Gerais.

The cowhide chaise longue near the little inner patio by the pool is by Le Corbusier (1887-1965).
The LC4 chaise longue, unveiled at the Salon d'Automne des Artistes Decorateurs in 1929, is the most famous of the furniture designs by Le Corbusier and the only one on which he worked personally. He called it the "resting machine." It is most remarkable that the resting position can be adjusted without any mechanism. Gravity simply holds it in place.

The home of Silvia and Roberto Moura was designed by Vianna and decorated by Silvia herself. The house, with V-shaped pillars, establishes a dialogue between the texture of the wood and stone. The eucalyptus logs were treated using computer-assisted graphics by Tora Log Homes, specialists in wooden structures.

"My idea was to revisit the classical concept of log houses, originally created for the Scandinavian winters, and adapt them to the Brazilian climate. Since we don't get snow here, the project included big verandahs at the front of the houses, cooling and lighting the environment, besides providing a beautiful view of the surrounding valleys."

Flag Halyard Chair created in 1950 by the Danish designer Hans J. Wegner (1914-2007)

Since wood has thermal insulating properties, log houses help heat the interior in the winter and cool it in the summer. The interior design was done by Vivi Nabuco and the owners, Lucia and Márcio Rebello. The house is surrounded by glory bushes (*Tibouchina granulosa*), which blossom in the autumn.

The fireplace is set into the stone tower. A skylight and glass panels are located on the high ceiling over one of the living rooms. The interior is lit all day long by natural light, unlike the original Scandinavian log houses which have small windows and low ceilings.

The decals on the windowpanes are to keep birds from flying into the glass.

The log houses at the Provence Inn, in Brejal, in the mountains outside of Rio de Janeiro, are surrounded by aromatic herbs that scent the surroundings. They belong to Joaquim and Maria Lúcia Nabuco, who also designed them. The bathroom features an eighteenth century Italian bathtub sculpted in solid marble.

IMPRESSION

ST GARDENS

Vivi Nabuco
Sônia Infante
Antônio Azeredo

LANDSCAPE DESIGNERS

Paulo de Hungria
Machado

ARCHITECT

The gardens on the São Judas Tadeu Farm outside of Rio de Janeiro remind one of Monet's impressionist paintings.

They were conceived by VIVI NABUCO, the farm's owner. Two landscape artists helped make her dream come true. ANTÔNIO AZEREDO, under the guidance of the great Brazilian golfer Mário Gonzalez, did the golf course, and SÔNIA INFANTE created the gardens beyond the course. What used to be marshland was transformed into a marvelous garden.

The farmhouse was designed by architect PAULO DE HUNGRIA MACHADO and finished in terra cotta.

Sitting on one of the benches on the bridge in the middle of the golf fairways gives one an incredible feeling of inner peace.

The gardens on the São Judas Farm are seeped with an indescribable harmony. A lush green carpet unfolds before the house, as far as the eye can see.

The fabulous golf course created by Antônio Azeredo is traversed by ponds with canals crossed by poetic wooden bridges.

On the edge of the pond, a bronze deer gives the final touch to this harmonious visual composition. Beyond the golf fairways and near the Atlantic Forest surrounding the property, landscape designer Sônia Infante drew inspiration from Monet to create a lush garden with indigenous Brazilian plants.

"The first time I saw that piece of land, I could feel it claiming to become a golf course."

Vivi Nabuco

WATERCOLOR

Ronaldo Fontainha

ARCHITECT

Vivi Nabuco

INTERIOR DESIGNER

Fernando Chacel

LANDSCAPE DESIGNER

Angra dos Reis, with hundreds of islands and beaches, is a tropical paradise on the southern coast of Rio de Janeiro state. On one of the beaches, RONALDO FONTAINHA designed five cottages for his client VIVI NABUCO, who did the interior design.

Rather than building one big house, she preferred to have five small, cozy cottages, providing greater privacy for her guests. All the original trees were preserved, and the cottages were built high above ground in order to minimize interference with nature.

The houses are interconnected by winding paths, creating enticing spaces between them that contribute to the overall harmony of the property.

View of the cottages as seen from the boat when arriving by sea.

The infinity edge on the tear drop pool appears to flow right into the sea at Angra dos Reis.

The façades of the houses were designed by Ronaldo Fontainha with works of art and ceilings created by local artists. The architect Sylvia Moura collaborated with Ronaldo Fontainha to design the exterior windows.

The verandah facing the sea at Angra has a thatched ceiling made by local artisans from Ilha Grande, the largest island in Angra dos Reis. The object on the right is a *puça*, a wicker trap used by fishermen to catch small fish.

The houses are interconnected by winding paths.

Mosaic of a mariner's compass lit by the late-afternoon sun.

Windows brought from Bali, Indonesia.

FAMILY HOUSES by the SEA
Tropical
TROPICAL HOUSES
JOBIM
ARNO

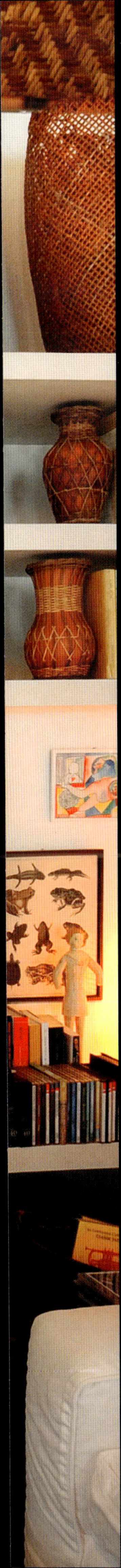

The smaller living room has a fireplace, a collection of baskets, round paintings by Marcia Grostein, and many books, since the owner is a publisher.

The living room of the main house features a skylight designed by Fontainha and interi design by Vivi Nabuco. An Indonesian daybed is flanked by light fixture made of coconu palm leaves. The plaited ceiling was made by artisans from Ilha Grande.

The woodcarvings of children carrying fruit, known as Black-a-Moors, were made in the "Oficina de Agosto" at the artists' community in Bichinho, Minas Gerais.

Umbrella stands.

The scenes on the armoire were painted by artist Ana Mello Franco and portray local scenes.

Door from Bali, Indonesia.

Mosaic of seashells on the kitchen floor in the "Pavilion."

One of the guest rooms in the "Pavilion."

Guest room with a stencil-carved wooden partition wall. The picture of the bird on the right is a cutout in the transom over the trelliswork.

Bathroom floor with a mosaic of seashells.

Bathroom sink by Mackenzie-Childs.

Always seeking to integrate home and nature, Fontainha incorporated natural rock from the landscape into the master bedroom's private pool.

"When you design a home in a place as marvelous as this, you shouldn't compete with nature. You have to join it."

Ronaldo Fontainha

The last house on the beach, a bungalow called the "Pavilion," was planned for guests. The façade is made of wood with carved-out stencil designs, and in the living room there is a boat-shaped bookcase.

OSSA NOVA

Façade of the home just a few meters from the Church of Santo Antônio.

BAROQUE I

NSPIRATION

Alcides da Rocha Miranda

ARCHITECT

Vivi Nabuco

INTERIOR DESIGNER

In the center of Tiradentes, an eighteenth-century heritage town in the state of Minas Gerais, renowned architect ALCIDES DA ROCHA MIRANDA (1909-2001) conducted the renovation of an old house near the Santo Antônio Church. One of his aims was to prove that one could live in an old historical house with all the modern amenities without disfiguring it.

Since the house is located in a preservation area, the old façade and part of the original tile roof were incorporated into the renovation plan.

From the outside it looks like a seventeenth-century house, but the interior has all the comforts of a modern home. VIVI NABUCO, the owner, did the interior design, using furniture and objects by craftspeople from Minas Gerais.

Front hall with the houses across the street reflected on the glass in the indoor patio.

"I don't see any contradiction between traditional and modern architecture. The old and the new can live together in harmony."

Alcides da Rocha Miranda

In the front hall, with a small indoor patio, antique objects blend harmoniously with more modern ones. For example, the eighteenth-century chair; the nineteenth-century console; the jaguar carved in Prados, Minas Gerais; and the modern painting by Luis Aquila, Rocha Miranda's son.

The largest of several interior patios was created by Rocha Miranda to light and ventilate the house, replacing the windows, which could not be placed on the side walls. A corridor with a view of the church tower connects the common area of the living rooms and kitchen to the bedrooms and bathrooms in the inner part of the house.

The historic town of Tiradentes, with the São José Mountains in the background, viewed from the Santo Antônio church tower. The roof of the house can be seen on the left.

"The reference to the Parish is a constant. Just two steps from the Church of Santo Antônio, the house fills its inner spaces with a golden glow, filtered by the yellow glass fanlights over the doors, evoking the gilded altarpieces of churches in Minas Gerais. Meanwhile, the roof garden unveils unexpected vistas of the church and bell tower."

Rocha Miranda turned the roof into a garden, taking advantage of the magnificent view of the church.

Dote

The bathroom has a wooden counter and bathtub, and an inner patio with a garden.

View of Rua da Matriz with the São José Mountains in the background. The house is the third on the left.

Façade in the evening. The evening lighting in Tiradentes comes from old streetlights, giving nighttime a romantic air. In the 1970s, Maria do Carmo Nabuco, the author's grandmother, was responsible for having all the utility posts removed from the streets. The electric wiring is now installed entirely underground.

23

Interior space in Rio de Janeiro created
Nabuco with the collaboration of Maria
Marcondes Ferraz. On the back wall is a
Ghost Dove from Tiradentes.

LANDSCAPE

The Museum of Contemporary Art is located on the Boa Viagem Lookout, on the coast in Niterói, a city that shares Guanabara Bay with Rio de Janeiro. The site was handpicked by Niemeyer while out on a drive in his car.

ART

Oscar Niemeyer

ARCHITECT

OSCAR NIEMEYER is one of the most important architects of our time. He was the first to turn reinforced concrete into art. In 1947 he designed the United Nations building in New York City, together with Le Corbusier. In the late 1950s he designed Brasilia, Brazil's new capital, which became a milestone in modern architecture. This book features one of his most beautiful works, the Museum of Contemporary Art (MAC) in Niterói, inaugurated in 1994. The museum's futuristic design, reminiscent of a chalice or flying saucer, blends perfectly into the landscape on Guanabara Bay, with Sugarloaf Mountain in the background. Niemeyer is now 104 years old and is still working on various projects around the world.

The MAC building itself is the first work of art that the museum offers to visitors for contemplation. The circular lines of the building's structure rise as a 16-meter-high (~53 feet) sculpture on an open square.

A winding outer ramp
leads into the museum.

Positioned on a rocky cliff, the museum challenges the conventional view by juxtaposing art with a panoramic view of Rio de Janeiro, daring visitors to see art and nature as one and the same.

"It's not the right angle that attracts me, nor the straight, stiff, inflexible line created by man. What attracts me is the free, sensual curve, the curve I find in my country's mountains, in the winding path of its rivers, in the ocean waves, in a favorite woman's body."

Oscar Niemeyer

The reflecting pool at its base gives the building an amazingly light feeling.

The modern architectural complex features bare, hard concrete with a rounded, smooth, and modern shape. This became Oscar Niemeyer's signature style.

Inside the museum visitors can enjoy the breathtaking view through a ring of windows.

I would like to thank everyone who helped in the making of these images, especially:

My aunt, Vivi Nabuco, who decorates her homes with amazing artistic sensitivity and greatly encouraged me to take pictures of architecture. My friend, and great artist, Hélio Pellegrino, who helped me see architecture as art. Deyse Krieger (my partner in love and art). My parents, Joaquim and Maria Lúcia Nabuco, and my brothers, Lourenço, Manoel, Mauricio, and Bernardo.

ARCHITECTS

Hélio Pellegrino: www.hpellegrino.com
James Lawrence Vianna: www.jameslv.com.br
Oscar Niemeyer: www.niemeyer.org.br
Ronaldo Fontainha: www.ronaldofontainha.com.br
Sylvia Moura

AND ALSO

Provence Inn: www.provence.com.br
Juice Co.: www.juiceco.com.br

Editora Bem te Vi: www.editorabemtevi.com.br
Oficina de Agosto: www.oficinadeagosto.com.br
Manoel Nabuco Advogados, Pedro Passos, Bruno Zeth, Lucia & Márcio Rebello, Roberto Moura, Hélio Vianna, Pérola Búzios Design Hotel, Patrícia & Marcelo Lages, Jupira Cabral, Tânia Lopes Gonçalves, Maria Mary Assis, and Cláudia Del Bene.

English Translation: Christopher Peterson
Photo Services: Sol Nascente www.solnascentebotafogo.com.br
Unimagem www.unimagemonline.com.br
Carvalho www.carvalhofoto.com.br
Eduardo Kubota

JOAQUIM NABUCO *is a Brazilian photographer who lives in Rio de Janeiro.*

He broke the family tradition of becoming a lawyer when he dropped out of law school to work as a photojournalist for some of Brazil's largest newspapers and magazines like O Globo *and* Trip.

In 1997 he opened his own studio in São Paulo and began collaborating with leading advertising agencies, fashion brands, and record labels.

In 2001 he moved the studio to Rio, returning to his hometown.

Nabuco believes that his key purpose in life is to publicize the beauty of his country.

He is also author of the Schiffer Publishing book, **BRAZILIANGELS**

To contact the author please write to jn@joaquimnabuco.com.br
See more of his photography at www.joaquimnabuco.com.br

Other Schiffer Books By The Author:

Braziliangels, 978-0-7643-3651-5, $50.00

Other Schiffer Books on Related Subjects:

Traditional Mexican Style Exteriors, 978-0-7643-1726-1, $39.95

Mediterranean Architecture: A Sourcebook of Architectural Elements, 978-0-7643-3891-5, $100.00

Contemporary Villas, 978-0-7643-3774-1, $59.99

Library of Congress Control Number: 2012931230

Designed by John P. Cheek
Cover design by Bruce Waters
Type set in ITC Avante Garde Gothic/Minion Pro

ISBN: 978-0-7643-4066-6
Printed in China

Schiffer Books are available at special discounts for bulk purchases for sales promotions or premiums. Special editions, including personalized covers, corporate imprints, and excerpts can be created in large quantities for special needs. For more information contact the publisher:

Published by Schiffer Publishing Ltd.
4880 Lower Valley Road
Atglen, PA 19310
Phone: (610) 593-1777; Fax: (610) 593-2002
E-mail: Info@schifferbooks.com

For the largest selection of fine reference books on this and related subjects, please visit our website at
www.schifferbooks.com
We are always looking for people to write books on new and related subjects. If you have an idea for a book, please contact us at
proposals@schifferbooks.com

This book may be purchased from the publisher.
Please try your bookstore first.
You may write for a free catalog.

In Europe, Schiffer books are distributed by
Bushwood Books
6 Marksbury Ave.
Kew Gardens
Surrey TW9 4JF England
Phone: 44 (0) 20 8392 8585; Fax: 44 (0) 20 8392 9876
E-mail: info@bushwoodbooks.co.uk
Website: www.bushwoodbooks.co.uk

Schiffer books may be ordered from your local bookstore, or they may be ordered directly from the publisher by writing to:

Schiffer Publishing, Ltd.
4880 Lower Valley Rd.
Atglen, PA 19310
(610) 593-1777; Fax (610) 593-2002
E-mail: Info@schifferbooks.com

Please visit our website catalog at ***www.schifferbooks.com*** or write for a free catalog.

Printed in China